Margaret & Bill :

Merry Christmas 1992!

Since this was my glorious trek this year, I wanted you to share the beautiful sights!

Much Love to You Both!

Jewell & Bruce

Familiar?!

GRAND CANYON
A PICTURE MEMORY

Text
Bill Harris

Captions
Louise Houghton

Design
Teddy Hartshorn

Photography
Colour Library Books Ltd
FPG International

Picture Research
Annette Lerner

Commissioning Editor
Andrew Preston

Publishing Assistant
Edward Doling

Editorial
Gill Waugh

Production
Ruth Arthur
David Proffit
Sally Connolly

Director of Production
Gerald Hughes

Director of Publishing
David Gibbon

CLB 2511
Color separations by Scantrans Pte Ltd, Singapore.
This 1990 edition published by Crescent Books,
distributed by Outlet Book Company, Inc, a Random House Company,
225 Park Avenue South, New York, New York 10003.
Printed and bound in Italy.
ISBN 0 517 01753 9
8 7 6 5 4 3 2 1

GRAND CANYON

A PICTURE MEMORY

CRESCENT BOOKS
NEW YORK

President Theodore Roosevelt, who never saw a natural wonder he didn't like, said that the Grand Canyon was the one place in America that every American should see.

On the other hand, when the Federal Government surveyed it for the first time in 1857, the official report said:

"Ours has been the first and will doubtless be the last party of whites to visit this profitless locality. It seems intended by nature that the Colorado River along the greater portion of its majestic way shall be forever unvisited and undisturbed."

You can't please everybody. But how were they to know that one day people would be riding in rubber rafts on the Colorado's rapids just for the fun of it. Or that they'd be able to fly down into the Grand Canyon in helicopters. And they certainly couldn't have pictured a time when any but the most intrepid tourists would trek across the Arizona desert on horseback just to see a hole in the ground. Even a hole as spectacular as the Grand Canyon.

Yet, taking President Roosevelt's advice, more than four million people walk up to the rim of the Grand Canyon every year. Some even climb aboard a mule and ride down to the bottom of it. And each and every one of them agrees that it is probably one of the greatest experiences of their lives, and certainly one of the most unforgettable.

An important part of the pleasure that the Grand Canyon gives visitors lies in the knowledge that it is a spectacle their descendants will also be able to enjoy. In a changing world, nothing seems quite as permanent as the Grand Canyon. It's been there for 600 million years, and though the Colorado River is working as hard as it ever has to change it, it isn't a job that will be finished any time soon. The bottom of the canyon is 2,000 feet above sea level, and the river will keep up its work until it is that much deeper, about half as deep again as it is now. At that point, the force of gravity will turn the mighty Colorado into a sluggish stream, but even then its handiwork will still be there. Considering that it took 400 million years for the river to cut through the much softer first 2,000 feet, if you don't get there this year or next, it probably won't make that much difference.

Except that a visit is not an experience that should be postponed.

The average Grand Canyon visitor seems to miss a great deal of the spectacle, however. The people who keep track of such things say the length of a typical visit to the park is three hours. According to the people-watchers, most visitors spend half an hour looking out over the rim and the rest of the time looking through the gift shop. Some, they say, miss the canyon completely, but they do seem eager to line up outside the park's South Entrance at the bustling little town of Tusayan to sit through a giant-screen movie of what they could see in person a short distance away. How it is possible to miss a 300-mile-long gash in the earth that's a mile deep and a dozen miles wide is hard to imagine. If these reports are true, they are also very sad.

Some visitors, they say, express disappointment that there is no elevator to get them down to the bottom. But others, with a spirit of adventure and a little foresight, arrive with advance reservations to ride down on the back of one of the 130 mules who are in the employ of the Fred Harvey Amfac Resort Company. The mules have made the trip so often they could do it with their eyes closed. They don't, but quite a few of their riders have been known to close theirs often on the way down. Most of them have never ridden a mule in their lives, and it's a strange experience even on level ground. Many of them are a bit queasy about heights, too, and the animals seem to get a kind of perverse pleasure from exploiting that fear. It isn't that the mules are mean-spirited, but they do enjoy grabbing an occasional snack as they go along. And if a succulent willow is close to the edge, well, who's afraid of a 500-foot drop? Actually, though the mules sometimes appear to be insensitive to the loads on their backs, they've been up and down the trail hundreds of times, and they aren't in the habit of losing customers for Fred Harvey, much less putting their own lives in any danger. The fact is, in fifty years of trudging up and down the trail, not a single mule has ever lost a rider.

The most common route taken by the mules is the Bright Angel Trail, which is an earthquake fault running diagonal to the canyon. It was beaten into a path over the centuries by animals in search of water and then by

Indians who farmed the pleateau known as the Tonto Shelf halfway down. It was further improved in the 1890s by a pair of promoters who said that they were planning to set up a mine in the canyon, but wound up mining the pockets of serious prospectors instead by charging tolls for the use of their road. Over the years since, the trail has been improved even more and these days features such amenities as telephones and drinking fountains.

The trip down the trail is a kind of history lesson. For the first 500 feet or so, the stone of the canyon's wall isn't much different from the surface. It is called Kaibab limestone, believed to have been formed from the sediment at the bottom of a prehistoric ocean that once covered this part of the Southwest known as the Kaibab Plateau. More accurately, it was two different oceans that created the top layer of gray limestone. The era that came between the disappearance of one and the creation of the next is recorded in a small, horizontal band of red stone.

That first 500-foot section represents a leap back to the Paleozoic Era, which predates the appearance of reptiles and, of course, mammals on the face of the earth. The next layer down was created during the Permian Age. It is a band of yellow sandstone about 400 feet deep, marked by undulating lines which were caused by the shifting sands of a desert. It took some thirty million years to create the yellow section, which rests on top of another layer of limestone that is called the "Red Wall." This is 550 feet deep and was built from the sediment of yet another prehistoric ocean, believed to have covered all of western North America for seventy million years. The band is red because the stone, originally gray, has been stained by iron deposits.

Not far below the base of the Red Wall lies the Tonto Platform, 3,200 feet down from the rim. This represents a sort of oasis among the rocks of the canyon, with trees and plants and a large spring that provides all the water for the village above. In moving between the Red Wall and the Tonto Platform, two eras of geological time have been lost, probably to erosion, but as the trail winds down further the history of the earth picks up again as if nothing had happened. The next section represents the remains of the Cambrian period, the era when one-celled animals began swimming in the seas. As the mule plods along, the rocks it kicks up are noticeably different from the ones on the trail above. They are much darker in color and their markings are strikingly different. Geologists call them Algonkian rocks and say that some of them date back to the Proterozoic Era, which began more than 250-million years ago. They are super-hard rocks with glittering traces of quartz in them, and were probably once the stuff of huge mountains that rose and fell long before life was any more than a dream.

Below that layer is yet another, made up of the oldest exposed rocks on the face of the earth. These date back to somewhere in the neighborhood of 4,600 million years ago, to a place in time known as the Archean Era.

If the mules have been trudging through a time machine, the adventure is far from over when they get you to the bottom. The trip down takes four to five hours, just enough time for travelers to get stiff from all that jostling and to begin to notice an odd feeling in their right hands, which have been pressed tightly to the saddle pommel most of the way. They haven't been able to see much of the river on the way down, but at this point it is in almost constant view as the mules wander along the almost level section of the Kaibab Trail, which merges with the Bright Angel Trail near the canyon's floor. When the trail was blasted out of the rocks in 1928, a 420-foot suspension bridge was built across the river at the same time. It leads to the Phantom Ranch, a comfortable place, not at all as primitive as one might expect, considering the location. The victuals are good and the water from Bright Angel Creek, which rushes down through a side canyon to join the Colorado nearby, is icy cold and arguably the best drinking water available anywhere in the world. The folks who run the Phantom Ranch always keep washcloths chilling in the creek with which to greet their guests, a memorable treat for people who have just spent half a day in the hot sun on the back of a mule.

The setting of the Phantom Ranch is a good deal like a thousand other places in the West. It has a rustic barn of a dining hall, a Western-style bunkhouse where hikers can get a night's sleep before hitting the trail again, and stone cabins for the better-heeled mule train customers. It is hotter down there at the bottom of the Grand canyon than in almost any place east of Death Valley, but there are trees and flowers, and birds flying overhead. Nearby buttes and cliffs hide the canyon's walls except in a few places, and it isn't until you realize that your car is a mile away ... straight up ... that you remember where you are.

And where you are is a place of splendid isolation. It is a place worth exploring, worth strolling through to the river to marvel at its incredible force, or to stick a toe into the frigid, unbelievably clean water of Bright Angel Creek. There are side canyons that provide inspiring vistas, and the fifty-foot-high Ribbon Falls, a five-mile hike from the Ranch, where ferns have taken up residence in a spray-filled glen that makes you think of nothing quite as much as the Garden of Eden.

It's a place that nobody likes to leave. But when the time comes, the way up is usually via the man-made Kaibab Trail, which is two miles shorter, though steeper, than the nine-and-a-half-mile one nature created. That makes the trip back easier on the visitors, but the walk uphill tends to make the mules a little grumpy. The whole adventure, including an overnight stay at the Ranch and meals, costs in the neighborhood of $225. Reservations have to be made long in advance, and there are rules that restrict the trip to people more than four feet, seven inches tall and weighing less than 200 pounds, the latter stipulation possibly instigated by the mules' union. A one-day trip, to the Tonto Platform and back, costs about $65 and includes a picnic lunch. Or, if you prefer shank's mare, you can walk the trail to the bottom. But be warned, you're going to have to walk back up.

The less intrepid, and those who didn't plan ahead, usually confine their Grand Canyon experience to exploring the South Rim, watching the sunlight play wonderful tricks with the colors of the rocks, and shouting occasionally to see if an echo answers back. Almost everyone looks down and wonders what it's like at the bottom, but just as often they look across and wonder what's over there on the North Rim, and why all the human activity is confined to this relatively small spot.

The man they say started it all was John Hance, who arrived in the 1880s and set up a mining camp. Like so many others who followed him, he quickly discovered that though there were minerals aplenty down there, the job of getting them up over the rim was no fun at all. But Hance liked the place and stayed to become the first to welcome the visitors who arrived by stagecoach from Flagstaff. His camp, about twenty miles from the present-day Grand Canyon Village, became the official destination at the end of the two-day ride. Amazingly, it was a popular trip, and before long Hance had a competitor in the form of Pete Berry, who built a hotel at Grand View Point in 1892 to supplement his income from a copper mine. Berry eventually sold out to William

Randolph Hearst, whose mining interests had put him on a path toward making the Grand Canyon his own private preserve. And not long afterward, the property increased in value when the Santa Fe Railroad took over a line that had been built to serve the copper mines and connected it to its own main line. In 1904, the Fred Harvey Company built the El Tovar Hotel, and from then on there was no contest.

When the canyon became a national park in 1919 it was already served by the Santa Fe Railroad, which continued to deliver visitors there through to 1968. The line has been restored and recently began service with a vintage train making one trip a day from Williams, Arizona. But rail service has become as outdated as the 1910 steam locomotive that is making the run. People seem to prefer to drive there themselves, to fly in aboard a small plane or arrive in a big bus its operators never fail to call a "motor coach." Once inside the Park, where cars are prohibited from using West Rim Drive during the summer months, they board buses that are quaintly called "Harveycars." Americans, it seems, aren't too fond of taking a bus anywhere. But thanks to the railroad, the Village on the South Rim has long-since staked its claim as the best place to have your breath taken away by a view that nothing quite prepares you for.

It probably is the best place. The North Rim is about a thousand feet higher, and the view from it includes a background of flat desert country, which isn't as beautiful as the lush forest that surrounds you there. The view from the edge is to the west, which means that the interplay of sunbeams and rocks is better at sunrise. Over in Grand Canyon Village, the show is at its best at sunset, which makes experiencing it a little easier for people who have trouble getting their eyes open at six in the morning.

The trip to the North Rim takes you though evergreen forests and beside flower-strewn alpine meadows. Most people who make the journey have come around from the South Rim, and having come from the near desert conditions of the other side, they occasionally forget where they are. But suddenly, just as is the case on the south side, the canyon appears as if from nowhere and somewhere back in the depths of your mind you hear some dramatic chord of music.

The dropoff from the North Rim is not as sheer as on the other side, and the river below is five miles further away. The landscape there is dominated by Douglas firs, blue spruces and mahogany trees punctuated by groves of aspens, much more like a Rocky Mountain setting than the desert across the way. It is also broken up by a network of side canyons that are as dramatic as the Grand Canyon itself, except for their size.

Between the rim and the river below stands a series of buttes that were named, along with so many other features of the Colorado River, by John Wesley Powell, who led the first expedition down the river in 1869. It had taken his party three months to float down the river from Green River, Wyoming, and it took them three weeks to make it through the Grand Canyon itself. He recorded angry waves as much as thirty feet high, and at least one set of rapids that dropped eight feet in a third of a mile. The steep cliffs made portages impossible, and when they reached the other end of the canyon, he reported, "Our joy is almost ecstacy." During the trip, his thoughts must have turned to religion more than once, and the buttes seem to have reminded him of monuments to God in India and Siam. Shiva Temple is one of the biggest peaks in the group, rising 4,000 feet from the floor of the canyon, and its neighbors have such exotic names as Zoroaster Temple and Brahma Temple. But one of them has the all-American name of Uncle Jimmy.

This was named for James Owens, a local character who made his living leading cougar-hunting expeditions on the Kaibab Plateau. His most celebrated client was former President Theodore Roosevelt, who went on one of his safaris in 1913 and, as happens to everyone else, fell in love with the place. Legislation that led to the establishment of Grand Canyon National Park had been passed in 1908, at the end of Roosevelt's second term. It was officially opened in 1919, a few months after the Old Rough Rider died. Had he lived, he probably would have been there for the ceremonies. T. R. was a man of many enthusiasms, but a place like the Grand Canyon represents the grandest of them. When he said it should be on every American's must-see list, it was advice straight from the heart.

Facing page: the Abyss, at the head of Monument Creek. Overleaf: a view from Pima Point.

12

Mohave Point and Pima Point (below), easily accessible from West Rim Drive, are popular places from which to view the canyon. Pima Point is possibly the best vantage-point on the South Rim; the view takes in two sets of rapids on the Colorado River. Mohave Point also affords magnificent views (facing page top). The view (right) from just below Mohave Point clearly reveals the strata that form the canyon walls. John Hance, one of the old characters of the canyon, used to practice a trick on unsuspecting tourists on foggy days. He would impress sightseers by sporting a pair of snowshoes and "setting off" across the fog-filled canyon for the North Rim. Of course, he didn't actually go, but instead walked off in the direction of Yaki Point (facing page bottom), from where he claimed the journey was considerably shorter. "You just keep watching and tonight when you see a fire over on the North Rim you'll know I made it," he used to say. The fact that snow shoes (with which to walk upon the fog) weren't easily come by in the canyon in the late nineteenth century seems to have prohibited anyone from following in his footsteps. Naturally there was often an obligingly imaginative tourist who would "see" the fire and if they didn't, well, there was all that fog wasn't there? Overleaf: a view from Pima Point.

13

Yavapai Point (below) is well worth visiting at sunrise when the first rays of the Arizona sun are just beginning to gild the upper reaches of the canyon and hint at what lies in the depths a mile below. Left: a low sun over a view from Hopi Point casts a mellow light on the scene, while (below left) the cold light of day reveals the crisp definition of the rock features seen from Mohave Point. Bottom left: Wotans Throne and Vishnu Temple silhouetted in the last light of day. Overleaf: daybreak at Hopi Point.

"There is a certain malady, commonly termed 'big head,' with which a large number of otherwise healthy people are afflicted. Prescription: stand on the brink of the Grand Canyon, gaze down, and still further down, into its awful depths, and realize for the first time your own utter insignificance." So said Mrs. Mary Hart of Maryland in 1895. Anyone suffering from this unfortunate defect might find Mrs. Hart's cure by gazing at the views (bottom right and overleaf) from Hopi Point or (right) from Mohave Point Lookout and (below right) beyond. Below: layers of red rock seen from Bright Angel Trail.

It was about twenty-five million years ago that the Colorado River (these pages) started creating the canyon out of the Kaibab Plateau. Two-hundred and seventy-seven miles of the river, which drops at a rate of nearly eight feet a mile and travels at a speed of four miles an hour, find their way through the canyon. The color depends upon rainfall and proportion of sediment and varies from toffee brown to jade green. Negotiated by many an adventurer, the river has also claimed many lives, its rapids proving extremely hazardous at times of low water. The Little Colorado River (overleaf) is sometimes tinted turquoise by a mineral spring upstream.

Bright Angel Trail (these pages and overleaf) starts from just outside the tourist village on the South Rim, where the visitor center (above) may be found. The mule trains favor this route, the sure-footed beasts tramping all the way down to Phantom Ranch. A rest-stop at the Indian Gardens (left), an area once cultivated by the Havasupai Indians, is customary along the way. The trail follows an earthquake fault as it bends and twists, sometimes even doubling back on itself (bottom left) in its effort to scale the canyon wall.

It's hard to imagine how the early explorers plumbed the unknown depths of the canyon – even harder once you've done so yourself. The trails today, although still demanding that care be taken, are well laid-out and maintained and the climb is much less arduous on the back of a mule. Walking is equally rewarding though – after all, it takes longer, so you're bound to take in more of the view! The South Kaibab (facing page top) and Bright Angel (remaining pictures and overleaf) trails, which converge down by the Colorado River, are the most well-trodden by those wishing to walk "down and up."

The views (below and overleaf) from Mather Point (left and facing page) take in a huge selection of the scenery offered by the canyon. Peaks, gorges, sharp cliffs, delicate curves, pastel tones, deep colors, light and shadow are all displayed here as they are nowhere else on earth. Mather Point is named for the first director of the National Park Service, Stephen T. Mather. The Grand Canyon was established as a national park in 1919 and the park was extended to almost twice its original area by an act of congress in 1975.

With rainfall on the South Rim averaging only about fifteen inches a year, the vegetation is limited to highly-specialized plants. Small, scrubby bushes and grasses survive in the arid conditions inside the canyon, while nearer the rim ponderosa pine may be found. Views (these pages) from and around Yaki Point show clearly how the landscape varies in appearance and harshness. Overleaf: "Duck on a Rock" Lookout.

The terrain varies considerably in the canyon, scrub and small trees covering some slopes (below left and bottom left) while only the sparsest life is supported by others. The nearest peak seen from Yavapai Point (below) is freckled with much greenery, while the distance is bare and barren. Temperatures in the canyon vary too; when there's snow on the Rim (overleaf) it's almost certainly been raining down by the river, part of which may be seen from Navajo Point (left).

Desert View Lookout is located about twenty-five miles outside the tourist village on East Rim Drive. Here the Watchtower (left and facing page bottom) is found, affording magnificent views (below) across the Colorado River. The Watchtower is an oversize replica by the designer Mary Jane Colter of prehistoric Indian structures found in the Four Corners region. The inside of the tower is decorated with authentic Hopi Indian murals which depict traditional legends and lend an unforgettable atmosphere to this convincing re-creation. To the east of Desert View lies the vast Marble Platform, along with Cedar Mountain, Echo Cliff and Navajo Mountain. The sun setting (facing page top and overleaf) over the canyon is an incomparable spectacle.

The varied and magical beauty that is the Grand Canyon has inspired artists and poets alike for generations. When Alfred Bryan, the popular songwriter of the early 1900s, visited the canyon he was moved to write a long and emotional poem that began with the lines: "I am the Grand Canyon, / My other names are Beethoven and Wagner, / Immortal as Sorrow, deathless as Love." Overleaf: the view from Navajo Point.

The Havasupai Indians, one of the oldest surviving tribes in America, still live in a village (above left) in lush Havasu Canyon (facing page, left, above and below left), forty miles northwest of Grand Canyon Village. Two miles south of the village lie the Havasu Falls (below and overleaf), set in beautiful, completely unspoilt surrroundings.

White-water rafting on the Colorado River is a marvellous way to see the canyon, the excitement of the ride adding to the glory of the scenery. Marble Canyon (facing page bottom, above and right) and the surrounding area (above right, below right and below) are best explored this way. Overleaf: Angel's Window. Following page: Moran Point, named for the nineteenth-century landscape painter, Thomas Moran, who practiced his art here.